11:11

Pamela Alvarez-Macabu

Charleston, SC
www.PalmettoPublishing.com

11:11
Copyright © 2022 by Pamela Alvarez-Macabu

First Edition

Paperback: 979-8-88590-271-7

Dedication

This book is dedicated to mom and dad and grandma. For being warriors. For all the sacrifices they made to give me a better life. For the dreams that all their children would make it one day. To my spirit guides, ancestors, whoever watches over me for the downloads, the signs, the constant pushes to keep going. And to all my readers who will come into contact with this book: I hope that my words, beautiful thoughts, and life experiences serve as the utmost inspiration to you. May this book inspire you find that light within.

Table of Contents

Love and Lust

We choose our lovers, and no one understands what we see in them but ourselves. No one understands what I saw in you, and that's okay because I experienced you in every way possible, in every frequency, through special little moments and traumatic ones too. Even when you showed me who you are, I still loved you despite your crazy, dark madness – for the simple reason that I always knew there was so much more beneath the surface. And because I loved you, of course.

I made the mistake of believing in your potential and hoping that it would be fulfilled with me one day. It's like I could intuitively envision who you were capable of becoming. Except you never could grow into that. Like a big baby, you were wounded and emotional, feigning to understand your pain. But you projected it in all the wrong ways. *We didn't know what to make of each other. You didn't know how to love a woman like me, and I didn't know how to deal with the darkness you held within.*

You were one of mine. One of those adventurous people – crazy to live, crazy to feel, crazy to escape. I always knew that there was a lovely soul beneath the surface. And I was tender for you. Not just because I wanted to fix you, but because I felt tied to you. It was the most electrifying connection I had ever felt. Maddening, cruel, and exciting all at once. Just know that I still think you are unique. And I still feel you. You had this vision, this way of viewing the world – a mixture of romanticization and jadedness. You had big ideas and a sensitive desire to change things. I was always amazed by just how much you contained on the inside – so much beauty, so much romance, so much hurt. You were dreamy. Full of illusions . . . and little did I know you were an illusion to me too.

Our relationship was characterized by small moments that, for me,
were really special.
And I just can't forget them.

I got fragments of you
in moments that will forever be imprinted in my memory.
Sadly, they were the only thing that made the experience
worthwhile.

I don't think there's any better feeling than being understood,
perhaps even better than being loved.
For someone to understand your behaviors, traumas, your quirks, habits, flaws,
understand your love language, how you process your emotions,
and still choose to love you, is priceless.

I sincerely believe there are people
in this world that you will meet
and with just a few encounters,
will love them inexplicably.
When you've crossed paths with a soul from a past life
you feel it.
Their energy is familiar to you.
It becomes so comfortable to be with them,
and loving them comes just as easily and quickly –
both lovers and friends alike.

That sensation of loving someone profoundly
that you can't even understand or explain it,
is so scary, isn't it?

Life is full of soul mates.
Your experience on this plane will be full of them –
life-changing encounters,
people your soul will instantly recognize.
Some will be sent to test you,
teach you lessons,
love,
or uplift and inspire you.

We made love
and still talked about it afterward.

The moon is full tonight,
and, as always, I think of you.

I believe in love at first sight
because there were people I met
and from the first interaction
I knew that I loved them.

I taught you that relationships can have depth. Your life was full of empty, meaningless flings until I came around and showed you that relationships could have a purpose. With me, you finally felt what it was like to be loved deeply. My intensity triggered you and is what ultimately drove you away. You didn't know what to do with the profundity of my love because you knew you didn't deserve it. You taught me all about a relationship such as ours – one to never tolerate ever again.

You were that love that I will never forget
not because it looked like a fairy tale,
but because it was toxic
and I learned a great lesson.

You broke my heart,
and I'll always remember you for doing that.
You'll be that love I tell my daughter when
she's suffering for an asshole like you.

I'm going to tell our story to teach her
to let go faster than I ever did
and to teach her what love is not.

I know that you have others
I know from the way you are on your phone.
Take it with you everywhere
as if your life depended on it
I feel it
and it hurts.
It always hurts.
Because my intensity and possessiveness
don't accept that you have others.
I want you all to myself.

Since you were an asshole to me
rest assured –
you will never have me like that again.

I want to be seen.
I want to be seen for who I am
beyond my looks,
beyond my body.
I want somebody to recognize my soul
and all the beauty within.
I want to be valued for that –
I am not a trophy.

lust

You realize it was not love
when the only good memories
you can think of
are the ones when you were having sex.

To all those people
I gave my body, time, and energy to:
You're welcome.
That was a fucking privilege.

I used to blatantly ignore the red flags in all my lovers
because I would get carried away by my emotions, the
chemistry I felt, my lust for them,
and convincing myself a connection was there.
Until I realized I was idealizing my father the whole time.
And that's why I idealized every man I ever fell in love with.

How ironic, isn't it?
Everyone's love life consists of short-lived love affairs
ridden with betrayal and toxicity.
We go through multiple disappointments in the hopes of
one day finding 'the one.'
We claim we don't want love
yet try to escape through another human being.
But more often than not,
no matter how good the love story,
even if only for a moment,
we find ourselves yearning for forever.
Wishing for that one person where it all finally clicks –
— *we're searching for love but still not ready for it.*

Sometimes we think we love someone.
But when we really think about it
we realize that
we are not happy for them,
or the new 'love of their life'
as they pretend.
That's how you know you loved them selfishly,
and that is not real love.

Don't dwell on what could
have been
if you had dated longer,
if you had met that person sooner,
if they hadn't ghosted you,
if you had communicated better,
or realized earlier you wanted something more serious.
The fact of the matter is,
it happened the way it was supposed to happen.
You saw their true colors,
and that's enough to know

it was not meant to be.

Pains

Demon time

You always used to call at 3 am,
and little did I know that was demon time.
And like the leech that you are,
merely called me over to pretend you like me,
to slide your hands into my panties,
touch my intimate areas,
whisper nasty little nothings into my ear,
And then proceed to take the most precious thing about me.
When you were done, you would send me on my way.

You always used to call at 3 am.
And little did I know you were just bored.
That I was, in fact, the 2nd, 5th, or 20th text message
You had sent that night.
And I accepted because you made me feel special.

You always used to call at 3 am.
Little did I know you would tease or abuse me
for your nightly entertainment.
Little did I know you did not genuinely like
or love me.
But my naivety and attachment to you
thought otherwise.

You always used to call at 3 am
because **you are a demon.**

Discarded.

You never gave a fuck about me.
That realization always formed a huge lump in my throat
that, for the longest time, was hard to swallow.
You never cared. Ever.
And that hurts my ego a lot more than it should.

Because I loved you profoundly,
and you felt absolutely nothing.
I was just a hot piece of ass to you.

I'll never understand.
I'll never understand how you can look at someone and
not feel anything.
How you can use someone's body and then discard it.
Because that's certainly how you looked at me,
with no feelings,
while my eyes sparkled at just the thought of you.

And when we fucked, I realize now,
it was for your mere pleasure.
And for myself?
Out of sheer love,
out of giving myself to you entirely.
I wanted to merge with you spiritually, emotionally, and
physically.
But you were empty,
with nothing to give,
nothing to offer.

You can't pour anything into an empty cup.
And, unlike me, you are content living that way,

by just taking, taking, taking
using,
and then disposing as if nothing.

Our wounds were similar, but we triggered each other.
You were intoxicating.
And I was merely your prey.

Long gone.

A part of me feels you are long gone.
A distant memory
I cling to
with the doomed hope
that someday you'll recognize me.
I want to have some sort of confirmation that you still
think of me,
or that you still care.

But at the same time, I realize you don't. You never did.
Its like I'm waiting for you to see my worth.
To recognize that maybe you felt some of the things I
did.
To feel wanted is better than to feel used.
Maybe having hope is better than accepting I was just
part of some sick, dirty game.

I'm starting to realize that it's simply who you are. You
never loved me or cared.
And probably go about your life without ever thinking of
me or regretting what you did.
You are too preoccupied with loving someone else or
fake loving them.
The truth I will never know.

Toxicity

The worst thing a woman can do to herself is to be in a
toxic relationship with a man.
An abuser will seek to diminish a woman's power.
He sees the potential
that she doesn't even see in herself.
He is aware of her beauty, intelligence, and power,
but he doesn't want *her* to see it,
As long as she doesn't see it,
he can keep putting her down.

It all starts when he begins to insult her ("are you dumb?"*)*
Degrades her ("you're a hoe"*)*
Calls her names ("you're ugly")
He sensed the weakness from the beginning.
He tested her boundaries
and she, unfortunately, failed.
Because if she loved herself
she would never tolerate abuse.
He will seek to have her in the palm of his hand
to break her
to the point of no return.
And after being put down so much,
sometimes, she will start to believe it.
Ladies, please don't wait until it gets drastic to leave,
and most importantly, love and respect yourselves.
Because a woman,
confident in who she is,
is an unstoppable force of nature.

Power

Abuse and an imbalance of power
characterize all toxic relationships.
Remember,
the abuser needs her.
He is obsessed with her.
Her energy is exhilarating for him.
He knows she is a good person,
and her aura speaks for itself.
It feels good to be around her.
But most importantly, he *knows* she loves him.
and he loves to be inside her,
because he feels just as good inside her
as beside her.

He knows she has no boundaries,
so he will keep hurting her
and inflicting pain to see how far he can go.
as if she were just a little experiment.
He'll keep her addicted by
'on' days
where he may treat her right,
and be affectionate,
until he gets comfortable again and begins to mistreat her.
The on and off, behaviors
have her searching for her worth *in his eyes*
instead of coming from *within.*

The only time he indeed knows how to please her
is during sex.
So, of course, she's hooked.
She's just as addicted to him
as he is to her.
She questions whether he loves her or not, but deep down,
she knows he doesn't.
Yet *she* loves *him.*
And that's enough, right?
He needs her
because she is easy –
easy to control,
easy to manipulate,
easy to hurt.
He needs her because
she doesn't realize her worth
and neither does he.

She is a true boss of a woman –
intelligent,
beautiful, and kind,
all that he wishes to be.
But she just doesn't know it yet.

She went a long time thinking it was love,
excusing his behavior
because he says he loves her,
or she thinks he gets jealous because he cares.
In reality, she formed an unhealthy attachment,
a trauma bond.
When she really thinks about it,
she doesn't have any good memories to reminisce about.
And when it seriously comes down to it,
she doesn't *want* to see him happy,
especially not with his new prey.
She is not rooting for them to be happy.
And if she can't be happy for him,
then she didn't truly love him.
She didn't know what real, true love was like because
she didn't even love herself.

Sometimes I look at how much I suffered
because of you,
but then I realize how much I've grown
and I have nothing else but to thank you.

Come Home

I feel bad for myself for missing him sometimes,
for having nightmares in which the only subconscious
desire I can pinpoint is his absence.
But then I realize that you are far lonelier
because you have a job you hate
and make barely enough to get by.
No one in your family gives a damn.
You live in a shack,
and go to sleep at night with the sound of guns firing
off in the distance, somewhere in the favelas.

And not even seeing you over the summer is enough
because time is short,
and there's nothing more painful than the inevitable
pain that distance will tear us apart once again
when we board that plane back to New York.

Maybe nothing will be the same.
Distance is so strange,
it tells us we love each other.
But we learned to live without you.

Our family is broken
and I doubt that we could ever really pick up the pieces
from where we left off.
We've adjusted to life without you
(or haven't we?).
Forgetting is always going to be a threat
or apathy.
Maybe I will never forget
but mom is tired of waiting.

You've missed my sixteenth birthday,
and you're going to miss graduation.
Those days were and will be
both happy and sad
just as things always seem to be.

We all pretend we don't miss you
and hide our emotions.
But now I don't even know what I feel anymore.
I thought this would be a poem
but it seems every time I try to write about the greatest pain
in my life,
nothing can do it justice.

11:11

Every time I came across those numbers,
my wish was for my father to return
so that my family can be reunited again.

And now that the time is finally coming,
I can't help but reflect on how much that may or may not
impact our family dynamic
the way I always dreamed it would.
Unfortunately, this wish does not denote everything
going back to normal.

It took me being in an abusive relationship to learn
what not to tolerate and look for in a man.
I found myself resting my head on shitty men's chests
who repeatedly looked for me in the middle of the night,
and calling it love.
Because any male attention was enough for me
when I was trying to fill that void.

And the middle one is so damaged
when I think about it –
the ADHD, the anger problems, the resentment,
smoking at a young age.
The lack of respect that will not go away easily
because his idol failed him. His father left him in his eyes.
And who was there to teach him how to be a man?
He had to learn by himself.

And the youngest was deprived of a father figure in the early years of his life.
Perhaps he'll have a figure to guide him through adolescence,
but he is also irrevocably a momma's boy.
Some think he may end up resenting you worse than the middle one.
So at this point,
what purpose does this serve?
Have I wished upon this for years for nothing?
The damage has already been done.
The growing has already been done
and some of the healing too.
Our family is irrevocably broken
and your return will not change that.

As the years go by
(and I can see them
by the wrinkles on your face)
you're still the same
handsome and dignified man
I've known all my life.
And I hope that one day I'll find someone
who's half the man that you are.

Often I am told that I have beautiful eyes,
and little do they know I get them from you.
Those same eyes I've seen cry.
Those same eyes I've seen flash with anger,
pain, and sadness.
The one thing I think I got most,
is your sensitivity.
I've seen the way you hurt when you witness the cruelties
of life
and I think,
Gosh, that's where I get it from.

Photographs

We communicate through texts,
but what impacts me most are not the words, but the
photographs.
When I see how you're balding
and the lines forming around your eyes
that weren't there when last I saw you,
I think, *Where has time gone?*
In all that lost time and space,
you're getting old and going through life
without us.
So many moments and opportunities for us to create
new ones –
gone.

While everyone else called you out,
while everyone else saw you for the mistake you made,
and insistence on leaving despite the challenges,
I defended you.
Until I finally saw what my mother and brother were
talking about.
That's when I took you off the pedestal.
I realized that I was idealizing you for being the good
father you always were to me as a child.
But you made your mistakes.
You were selfish, stubborn,
and didn't do much to change your situation or your
negative, unrealistic mindset.
And the worst part is that you immediately sensed the
energy shift,
almost as if I was the only one
easy to manipulate,
the only one who was still blind.
All this time I realized I was only focusing on the good
things I saw in you –the good childhood memories.
But eventually I had to confront your mistakes, your
faults,
your toxic traits.
And it was I who had to have those painful conversations.

Nostalgia

Life is like a passing film.
People that come and go
serving either as a lesson or an experience
(or both).
But at some point, everyone and everything becomes a
memory
that may replay in your mind – especially
in those moments when you are
feeling particularly nostalgic.
Or it will fade away to some distant part of your brain to
the point of indifference.
And you see, my only problem with that is,
some moments and some people are just too precious
I wish I could stop the time
or go back so that the feeling can last forever.

Issues

I've always been that friend who always appeared strong
and to have it together,
sweet with a big heart, but only once you get past the icy,
standoffish exterior.
I've always been the friend with the soundest wisdom,
who will always encourage you to do the right thing and
take the high road.
But no one questions where this wisdom comes from.
No one knows of the pain and trauma
because I buried it so far within me.
I may appear to be wise and have it all together, but come
to think of it –
I have issues.

Healing

Don't try to understand why he didn't love you.
He simply couldn't.
Because he saw no value
or worth
in keeping you in his life.
But mostly, he didn't know how to love someone like you.
Know your worth and move on.

Growth

I read somewhere that it takes about two years to get over a heartbreak.
We are sensitive beings,
so when we put all our love and trust in a lover or a friend, who betrays us,
it hurts. Especially when they do you unbelievably dirty.
The first man I happened to get involved with and lose myself to,
hurt me profoundly.
It took a solid year and a half to two years to get over that painful situation,
and no, it did not take meeting someone new to get over that.
I learned what it was like for a man to treat me nice,
but those love interests came and went.
In the end, what saved me,
was my own self-love and healing.
It meant learning to love and respect myself,
build confidence,
trust my intuition,
and never ignore the red flags,
to look past the physical and into people's hearts –
their morals, their values, how they were raised,
how they make your nervous system feel.
Do they take you seriously,
do they help you grow, expand your mind,
bring light to things you need to keep working on

or have traits you wish to have yourself?
It took time to learn to be alone,
so that my happiness may never depend on another
human being.
I discovered how peaceful my presence is
how calm it is to belong deeply to myself
and not have my energy tainted or absorbed by anyone else.
I learned to have boundaries when it comes to having
access to my time and energy.
I learned to have standards and honor them.
I learned that my body is sacred, and so is my mind.
For me to share my gems,
someone must meet my vibration.
That's when healing is a beautiful thing
because you help better yourself for yourself.
By no means is it an easy feat –
it means losing people,
their true colors being exposed to you,
growing apart because your growth does not match
theirs.
It means starting all over again
to make space for people and things that are in alignment
with you
and your newfound growth.

A pivotal turning point in healing
is when you look back
and wonder how you ever tolerated what you did.
You'll feel resentment towards that person and
get angry at yourself for having been so stupid.
Mad for the times he treated you like shit,
for the times he laid a hand on you,
manipulated,
gaslighted,
lied,
and called you names.
You will resent him more than you ever loved him
but that's all part of healing.
Feel it out.
And **forgive yourself.**

Healing from a toxic relationship is coming to terms
with the fact
that you attracted such person
because whether you want to admit it or not,
they were a reflection of yourself
and the frequency you were vibrating on.
They mirror back the good and the bad.
A turning point is realizing that
you are a good person, but there are dark, unhealed parts
within you,
and that is okay. Because we are all human and have our
traumas.
We simply must come to terms with it and have the self-
awareness to change and become better
for ourselves. Remember to hold yourself accountable.
And find all the strength and self-love within to heal
yourself.

As we heal from people and situations we come to terms with the fact
they came into our lives for a
reason.
We simply must take the lesson and move on.
Accept that a part of you can still love them and want to see them happy
-just from a distance.

We grow apart from certain people
because the part of ourselves that connected with them
no longer resonates with their energy.

The first step is recognizing our problems
and flaws.
What you do to fix,
heal,
or better them,
is up to you.
-awareness

vulnerability

We live in a world
dominated by appearances.
We feel we have something to prove,
show how happy we are,
how good we look,
how much money we make,
what a great relationship we are in,
and try so hard to entertain an audience that doesn't even
exist.
What we project is not an accurate depiction of our
reality.
Most of the time, we are not even truly happy.
But what does that matter if other people fall for it?
We are scared of being vulnerable.
We mask our pain
because subconsciously
we feel some type of way about it.
We choose to be private and secretive about
the real things we go through,
the dirty, gritty painful realities and problems.
Because we feel that if people were to know,
they are going to judge.
We choose to conceal our pain
because we are ashamed of it.
Somewhere in the back of our minds,
there is some negative emotion
regarding the things we go through,
our emotional wounds.

We live in a society
that strives for perfection.
Except, no one has a perfect life,
a perfect relationship,
a perfect body.
All of that is relative and subjective.

Usually, the ones who appear to have it all, don't.

Life, like us, is flawed.
So when we deny our realities,
we close our hearts and
choose to live in fear of getting hurt.
We close the door to endless opportunities.

Don't be ashamed of what you've been through
because those things don't define you
and every day that you wake up
you are given another chance at life.

It takes real bravery to be able to own up to it.
Once you do,
you are erasing feelings of shame.
No one can shame you on something
you are not embarrassed about.

And once you do that,
you get one step closer to sharing your light.

Remember, the right people won't use it against you
or judge you.
They will love and admire you despite it all.

It took me years to find the courage and strength to put my work out there.
There were times when certain experiences were still so painful
I couldn't bring myself to write about them.
And that's okay.
There will come a time when you will feel ready to confront that pain
and not only that, but understand it, heal it and overcome it
— *Some things are still just too painful.*

It hurts when you realize
you didn't mean as much to someone
as they did to you,
when you grasp they never truly cared,
that you were not as unique to them as
they were to you.
But never question why God removed someone from
your life.
He felt intentions that were not genuine.
He dismissed those whose energy was only
going to keep you down
It hurts, I know.
But don't hold yourself back by clinging to low
vibrational energies
that do not truly love or support you
The last thing you need is to block your blessings.
And remember, the most important lesson to be
learned is
that the hurt was necessary.
It was necessary to give you that moment of clarity
as to who they really are and why they don't belong
in your life anymore.
That in itself is a blessing.

You ignore the red flags for the sake of lust
or because you feel a connection.
You ignore the red flags
because you choose to see the good in people.
But understand that when you do so
you betray yourself,
your intuition,
your self-respect,
and your intelligence.
Take people off the pedestal,
see them for who they are.
That way, you're not naively shocked
when they do you dirty.

Just a reminder that you are not your past,
your pain, or your traumas.
You are who you choose to be today, tomorrow,
and every day of your healing.
You decided to be a better you.

New Beginnings

Whatever it is you do –
that project you're working on
the business idea that's been planted in your head,

just start. Work hard and give it your all
until it's the best you possibly could have done.
When you do something in alignment with who you are,
the Universe will support and bless you abundantly.

Everything comes full circle.

There is no age or number to measure success.
Everything happens according to divine timing.
Don't stress that you haven't achieved what you wanted to
at the time you thought you would.
Sometimes the Universe shows us what we are capable of
or gives us a glimpse of it,
but it won't manifest until the time is right.
In the meantime, you still have things to heal,
inner work to do, negative energetic chords to let go of.
Not to mention the countless trials, tests, and tower
moments
the Universe will put you through
just to prepare for the moment when your manifestations
come true.

Be light

Be the light God that gave you
because you were born to share it with the world.
Whether your affinity is singing, cooking, writing,
painting,
when you share it with the world,
you are shining that bright light within.
And whether you realize it or not, you are making an
impact
and fulfilling your purpose.
You never know how much you can inspire someone.
We all have gifts to share with the world.
We can all be inspirational.
There is no talent
superior or inferior.
Your light is yours,
and no one can take it away.

In the end, what attracts people is energy.
And someone whose intentions are always pure,
and transmits good energy,
will always shine brighter than others.

Be careful what you wish for
because the Universe will conspire to make it happen
and you won't even see it coming!

I am a poet
because poetry has no limits or boundaries.
It is free,
like me.

There will be people who will envy you
because they wish they had the same heart,
the magnetism, charisma you possess
and an aura as illuminating as yours.
They wish they had your *essence.*
Your job is never to take it personal
because the ones who get triggered
are the ones unaware of their power.

You are one of those girls
(one can just tell),
is a beautiful soul.

With a captivating smile
and looks that kill –
piercing, intense eyes that see right through everything,
but transmit innocence and sensitivity at the same time.

You are not just beautiful
for the way heads turn when you walk into a room. Your
aura and charisma speaks for itself.

When you smile, you never really know what she feels
because her eyes light up, so do yours just by looking at her.

But you can't see the sadness, the pain,
the traumas, and the stories that she hides.
You never know if she is happy or sad
because it's so easy to get fooled.

You are one of those intense women
not everyone can understand
or, unfortunately, love.

Whose inner beauty does not compare with the outer . . .
beautiful girl with the gorgeous smile
and innocent eyes.
You are *so* special.

When we pursue our passions, our purpose is being fulfilled
as well.
But when we deny them,
things never really seem to go right.
We constantly find ourselves hitting a brick wall.
Because when we run away from who we are,
and what we are meant to do
we are missing out on a bountiful life
where are all the right people and connections,
will fall into place.
And the sooner we realize that, the better.
Let go of fear, let go of doubt, let go of negative thoughts,
and feelings that may be holding you back.
Whatever you dreamed of,
whatever resonated within your heart and mind
was placed there for a reason.
Remember, you are the boss of your life.
You have the power to create whatever your heart desires,
and make the life you want to live a reality.
and the key is:
it is all within you.

All your gifts, talents, thoughts, and ideas
are enough to carry you through this world –
to make an impact,
to inspire others,
to build an empire for yourself.
You don't need to rely on anybody,
you don't need people to support you,
you don't need to depend on a system
or be enslaved to it.
You are greater than that.
You are enough.
You have thousands of angels and ancestors guiding
every step along the way,
creating miracles,
opening and closing doors to pave the way for you.
Success is yours.

Once you step into your power as a woman,
you are unstoppable.
Never apologize for being too much,
for the way you carry yourself,
for occupying too much space,
for being fierce, headstrong, demanding,
and knowing what you want.
Your confidence and power will always threaten people
who can't recognize theirs.

I used to pray and write in my manifestation journal
that I wanted to experience more people and things.
I wanted to venture into falling in love more,
having had those idealized, short-term relationships that
start off exhilarating and then destroy you just as quickly.
I felt I needed to fall in love again,
especially after I had my heart broken and been single
for so long.
I thought I needed the inspiration and newfound pain or
obsession for my art.
Or to lose myself in another human being to write,
but then I realized that those are merely distractions.
I am enough.
All the inspiration is within me.
All my beautiful thoughts, feelings, and ideas are
more than enough to inspire –
and more than enough to be my art.

Never underestimate your ability to impact
and inspire others.
It doesn't matter how long you've known them –
you could have shared one night or only two moments
with them.
Yet they could have had an incredible impact on you
and vice versa.
—*Two dates in, and you triggered me enough to go back
to therapy.*

serendipity

There are people you attract according to your energetic vibrational frequency, but the best kinds of people come into your life as a pure act of fate.

They say New York is a world,
but in reality, it's just full of millions of people,
all broken in some way –
damaging the other,
trying to survive,
trying to make it.
It's the type of place that forces you to become selfish,
cold and heartless,
sometimes for survival,
sometimes as a form of protection,
most often, both.
But when you take a moment and get to know people, you
realize everyone has a story.
And somewhere along the line, after multiple
disappointments,
heartbreak,
toxicity, generational traumas,
the illusion of endless options, constant search for
something better, the inevitable competition
and secret animosity that exists in a city like this,
you just close your heart off.
It is not until you get out, travel, and see how other
people live
that your perspective on life changes.
Only then will you understand what it means to live a
meaningful life.

Jungle girl

I am a jungle girl.
Because just like the jungle,
I am a storm
and a paradise
at the same time.
Like the weather,
I am temperamental.
One day I can drown you in tears
or burn hotter than the sun.
No forecast
can predict what you're going to get from me.

Not everyone is going to be impacted by the same things as you.
Sometimes you have to keep certain things to yourself because not everyone has the depth or capacity to appreciate them as you do.

I romanticize things
because in my head
they are much better realities to accept.

Animal and children lovers

Behind every person who 'hates people,'
is a compassionate individual.
One who probably got hurt and betrayed
by other humans.
Who, somewhere along the line, lost a certain degree of
hope for humanity.
And finds solace in the innocence and harmlessness
of animals and children.

And when I had no other choice
I simply had to let my words bleed on the page.
They are my only solace
in this greedy, cruel world.

When I have no one to turn to,
when I feel like no one would understand,
when I feel like suffering alone
because no one is worthy of hearing about my pain
or knowing my vulnerabilities,

the only option I ultimately have,
is to pour my heart out
on the page.
My writing is my art.
I find comfort in knowing
that my problems won't fall on nosy, uncaring ears.

That I don't have to call or text someone
who may not have my best interests at heart
because maybe I didn't know them as well as I thought I did.

Oddly enough, my solace comes from putting it down
on paper, what no one else could see
hoping to feel better about my problems.
It is just for me.
A secret between my journal and I.

I want this to be the most beautiful recollection of me,
So that my most beautiful thoughts and feelings,
may be imprinted in people's minds.

Hero

Never look for a savior outside your life.
No single person or entity will save you –
no government, politician, employer, friend, or family.
When you've lost all,
the only person who can make a difference for yourself,
is *you*.

Lovers worth writing about

This chapter is dedicated to better people and things
because shitty people don't deserve any more of my
words,
and much less any more pages in my book.
This is my life
and you will no longer take up any space in it.

-Bye

Enzo

I remember when we met
it was one of those things
where the attraction was immediate,
and, of course, it happened in the summertime –
early June, to be exact.
And of all places, in my own neighborhood.
I remember walking into our section at the nightclub.
As you were being escorted out,
I brushed past you.
You looked back to stare at me,
immediately taken aback.
You wanted to say something but couldn'tas your friends
tugged you away.
And throughout the night
I would steal glances at you
to see what you were doing,
who you were dancing with.
I would report your whereabouts
to my girlfriend who was with me that night.
We would both refer to you as
"That cute, white boy."
The attraction was there, but my awkward self
didn't know what to do about it.
And so when we finally left,
you happened to be outside with your sister and her
friends
waiting for your ride.

We made eye contact as I walked away
except
you were too cute for me to miss the opportunity.
So I pretended to look for a lighter in my bag
with a cigarette pressed to my lips.
Eventually, you came up to me,
asked for my number and told
me, I was gorgeous.
And on the inside, as awkward as I am,
was unable to express how flattered and happy I felt.
I could merely smile and put my number on your phone.

I asked how old you were.
When you told me you were 23,
I was a little surprised you were only a couple of months
younger than me.
I remember your sister called out to you in French as she
and her friends piled in the uber.
"I'll be right there," you called to her,
and as you walked away
"I'll text you."

Later that evening, I got, "Hey, it's Enzo, just so you
have my number. I really want to take you out sometime
if you're willing. It'll be fun." :)

You know how men always have that one good woman they regret fumbling?

And they live with that regret for the rest of their life
because what kills them the most is that they had a good thing.
It could have been a better relationship than it was,
and that's exactly how I felt about you.

You kept me on my toes
and always checked to see when I was available.
You never told me what the plans were,
only that you would let me know what you came up with.
So the whole week leading to our date
I did not know what to expect.
You were a true romantic.

On our first date,
I didn't have too many expectations.
I was obsessed with someone else at the time
who wasn't giving me any attention.
So you were just a second option.
But when I saw you greet me outside that restaurant in Green Point,
I was stunned.
You looked so handsome
and well kept.
I remember internally screaming and texting my friends
about how I couldn't believe this was real.

There weren't any tables available
So, we sat at the high tables before the glass walls
facing the streets of Brooklyn
with its outdoor dining.
You sat directly beside me

in your khaki pants, white tee, pullover on top,
raven curly hair and bluish grey eyes.

I couldn't believe it.
I felt so lucky that we crossed paths.
You were so charming but in the gentlest way
You wore these silver bands on
your crafty hands,
and I could never forget how
it complimented them so nicely.

When you got hot, took off that pullover sweater and I
saw how those chains dangled on your neck,
I knew I wanted them dangling in my face that same
night.
The jewelry you wore gave you a subtle little sex appeal
that was irresistible,
and I loved to hear the stories of how they were passed
on from your grandparents.
You had a deep appreciation for them, and that is
something
I loved that we both shared in common.

I learned that, as opposed to me, you didn't have much
going for you.
Came from money, were a college dropout
who would occasionally help with your parents' business,
and you had your cool marketing job.
But to me
you were a real gem
because you were raised right,
always respectful, always a gentleman.
And at the time, I suppose I thought that was ideal.

I remember when we snuck into your grandmother's basement
at her house in Forest Hills.
How you led me to the creaky old staircase
and into the basement,
how we sat on the couch
and you had your arm around me.
"This is it,"
you said.
I remember the tension, the excitement
the slow, awkward buildup,
how it started to escalate
as your hands slowly traveled from my arm
to my thick thighs
and squeezed my ass.

You loved the buildup, the foreplay.
Slow and steady,
although it was nice,
I got bored and took charge.
Sat on top of you,
flipped my hair to the side, and leaned forward to kiss you again.
You said, "You are trouble, and you know it,"
and I smiled because I knew.

My biggest regret is that we didn't get to spend more time together,
that I didn't get to share more moments with you,
and that I didn't get to know you better.
I regret being easy,
but I regret being prideful the most
because I didn't even wish you a happy birthday.
The moments we shared were very few,
but it was enough for me to know I had met someone special.
And I still wish we had more.

Maybe you were meant to be just another page in my book,
eternalized into a poem,
as a cherished memory and sentiment
– *nothing more.*

I may not be the firstborn in my lineage
but my ancestors did not endure
racism, slavery,
blood, sweat, and tears.
And my parents didn't immigrate
like star-crossed lovers
from two different
but neighboring countries
to come to the United States
as the first in their family.
They did not start from the bottom,
go through exploitation and discrimination
to make a new life for themselves.
I may not be the firstborn in all my lineage,
but I was the first to be born on this land.
I was born to be a trailblazer, to pave the way for
generations to come,
break generational cycles,
and build generational wealth for
myself and all my family to come.
— *Abundance is my birthright.*

A true queen does not need a throne,
castle, or riches
because a true queen shines despite those.
When you're in the presence of a queen,
you know it, you see it, you feel it,
and what do you do in the presence of royalty?
— *Bow down.*

Depth

I am a profound person,
an old soul
with a depth that not even the ocean could understand.
It feels lonely most of the time,
because I feel most people are not like this,
even if they are just as sensitive and intelligent as I am.

I take life very seriously.
I feel everything very deeply
and experience every sentiment to the fullest.
I can barely hold an easy-going conversation
because I see the deeper meaning behind what everyone says,
always reading between the lines,
and analyzing people.

That is why I am quiet.
I take in every person, every moment,
place,
and appreciate it.
It must linger and process in my heart and mind.

But then I remember my father
and how I got it from him.
Only you have that depth.
As I get older, I come to appreciate that in you more.
It's a strange thing
because we never need to recognize it.
We never even have to say anything.
We simply are.

We've always lived life like this
as if it were normal.
Only we know what it's like to live inside our minds.
Only we know what it means to be profound.

Spirit

How wonderful it must be to be a spirit,
able to live in various lifetimes,
in various dimensions,
omnipresent.
We value life so much on the physical plane because of
the things we can feel in the flesh,
but there is life after death,
Your spirit never dies and
neither does energy.
It will continue to live on
and be felt by those you watch over.
Our physical presence on earth is just felt in one lifetime
but on the other side
you get to watch and guide those who come next in your
bloodline.
That's why it is essential to give thanks to your ancestors,
to honor and pray to them
because their spirit will continue to live in you,
guide you,
protect you.
The way spirit follows you everywhere you go,
you can follow and guide your brethren
once you become an angel spirit.
And I think that's exceptionally beautiful.

-444

I've always been that girl with a unique perspective.
I just see things differently and more profound than most.
I think that's what people love most about me –
— *My mind is my superpower.*

Aquarius

I could never understand why anyone would be a
follower.
Why would anyone try to fit in and be accepted?
I could never understand the desire to conform.
I was meant to be the one who would question authority
and stand up for what is right.

I was not meant to be ordinary,
to live an ordinary life,
to base my opinions and thoughts on those around me
or the general population.
I don't care for social approval.
I don't want to be like the rest.
I want to stand out.
I want to be different.

I am the trailblazer,
the trendsetter,
the one everyone copies and admires.
I am the one who paves the way
and encourages everyone around them to embrace their
true selves.

I've gone through
moments of deep solitude and isolation,
mainly after every betrayal,
which only further reminded me –
I need to be comfortable being alone.
I've realized that I may be alone for the rest of my life
and that is okay
because friends will turn on me,
lovers may fall out of love with me,
and my own family may misunderstand me.
The whole world can turn against me,
but that's okay
because I will never abandon *myself.*
Spirit has continuously shown me that it's lonely at the top
and that I won't be able to handle success if I take things
personally.
I don't care if I'm the last one standing,
I will walk this world alone.
If it means standing up for my own beliefs,
I will always march to the beat of my drum.
And I shall live my life as I please.

Some things are just too beautiful to be captured,
neither by photographs nor poems.
You can try, but they just won't do them justice.
Like the moon, for example,
as soon as you turn your camera on,
it is incapable of capturing its beauty.
Sometimes the most attractive people are prettier in person.
The most beautiful things aren't meant to be captured.
They are meant to be experienced.

This year, more than ever,
God has pushed me
to find peace within.
This year, more than ever,
I've encountered more snakes in my garden.
I've learned that people will always turn on me,
but I must never turn on myself.

We met in Miami.

Our first date was on the beach.
It was perfect.
The waves, us exchanging ideas,
you, holding me in the water,
the waves hitting us ruthlessly,
my tiny bikini top falling off.
You, saying it was bizarre
that the waves were so violent
because the last time you came
they were so calm.
I thought it was very symbolic of the intensity
that would ensue,
including the passion that you and I felt
before anything even started.
I'm always taken aback
when I meet someone,
then something bizarre happens
and they says that doesn't typically happen to them.
It's like my presence alone brings turbulence.

I remember before we met
I felt super insecure.
I thought that I looked ugly,
my hair dirty,
the two hours of sleep visible on my face –
I tried to hide it with makeup.
But all of that came off
when we dove into the ocean.

From the start, you were seeing me in my natural form.

As we chit chatted under the sun,
talking about soccer, açaí, our outlooks on life
our families, careers,
everything flowed.
All the tiredness I felt went away,
you brought me energy
and I felt good.
We just clicked.
And it came so naturally.
Lying down next to you
was funny because we never actually made eye contact –
we just squinted our eyes at the sun,
and talked.
Occasionally stealing a side eye glance to each other.
We stayed for hours like that.
When we finally left
I felt renewed, like a brand new person.

Brickell

It is incredible how meeting one person
can catalyze change in your life.
We were walking through Brickell,
admiring how beautiful the glass buildings were.
"It's like a tropical Manhattan," I observed.
"Right! It's so beautiful here," you said, sipping on the
açaí smoothie that we had gotten for breakfast.
Peopled rollerbladed past us
or were running shirtless as we continued to take in the
beauty of Brickell.
"I think I'm just going to move here. It makes more
sense.
I spend the most time here anyways," you said.
I realized walking through those streets that I could see
myself living here too –
the way the beautiful glass window skyscrapers reminded
me of New York,
the palm trees, the hot sun,
how the weather was so lovely, it called for outdoor
workouts.
I could picture myself rollerblading in the tropical sun,
feeling the breeze run through my hair,
and the relaxed, easy-going energy.
It was just the vibe I needed.
And funny how we both decided at the same time.

We took different flights
but to the same destination.
Since I came home,
you never looked for me again –
never sent me a message,
never kept any of your promises.
I never felt so used in my entire life.
I would've loved it if we at least kept in touch
as friends.
But in so little time, you already hurt me.
I don't like to feel used and discarded.
You lied to me
when you spoke of all the things we were going to do
together
when we arrived in New York.
The worst part is,
I did it to myself.
In those first moments we met,
I could sense you were a little dangerous.
I knew from the start you were probably going to be the
one to hurt me.
You were like a dog with a spiked leash.
I knew I should stay away, but I couldn't.

You used me,
and once again, I felt like a clown.
And the worst part is, I didn't even expect it.
I felt so loved when you kissed my nose
and asked
"Are you okay baby?"
You were so nice to me
and made me feel so secure
like no one ever has.
I hate how easy it was…

December 12, 2021

Since 2019 I've been going through this cycle
of outgrowing relationships in my life.
Unfortunately
they were not peaceful outgrowings,
they manifested as betrayal.
The snakes I discovered in my garden
were always the ones closest to me.
They did not have my best interests at heart
and gossiped about every vulnerable thing I confided in them.
It seems as though every year someone new or two
betrayed me.
People I had the most history with
people I thought genuinely cared about me.
Each betrayal hurt just as deeply as the last
and traumatized me to the point of detachment.
So, for two years, I've been in this endless cycle
of finding myself,
healing myself,
and growing out of people.
But the whole time, I didn't realize that I was growing
out of my own city.
I've always heard that growing out of places is a thing,
but I never quite experienced the feeling.
that every single time I left New York since 2020,
I would cry as soon as I landed back.
And so, on December 12, 2021
when it was time to leave Miami after a magical weekend,
I finally realized that my love affair with New York was
ending.
And that was the most toxic one in my life,
more harmful than any friendship or relationship.

It was through travel that I realized what it means to live to the fullest
and what a good quality of life is.
I realized that working hard and commuting with the utmost stress
to pay bills or be a slave to a system, is not it.
I realized how weather impacts your mood,
that I wasn't built for brutal, cold winters
or people who are insensitive,
competitive and always looking for something better.
I belong someplace tropical where the force of nature alone
lifts my mood,
where my heart is much more open.
Over the years, it began to develop into a love-hate relationship
with this damn city,
which was very odd,
since it was always love.
I would rep New York like it was my nationality.
It was where I always said I'd spend the rest of my life.
That's the curse of being from New York –
you can never picture yourself living anywhere else.

I'll be New York till I die.
This city, like all my past lovers,
will always have a place in my heart.
But now it's time to end this toxic love affair.

We had the type of friendship that no one would understand.
You are crazy, unconventional, and adventurous, a real trip, and you bring that out in me.
You bring the excitement and adventure I've always sought in my life.
You live your life as you please, no fucks given
because you genuinely don't care about societal norms, and you don't value all the same things most people do.
You do what people WISH they dared to do. And that's why they admire you so much.
You just keep doing you,
completely unbothered, unhinged, a true free spirit.
You're an artist, so you get it.
And that's why we clicked.
From the first link,
I was inspired to hear how you made a living off your art, how you envisioned it,
and how you manifested it all.
You were persistent and never gave up on yourself.
That got me thinking about how success would find me, too, through my art.
You really inspired me.

Transformation

You can shed old layers
and kill the old parts of yourself
to become a new, better version.
It's like getting a fresh, new chance at life.
And I think that's really beautiful.

The old you
didn't honor, love, or respect yourself enough.
But that's all in the past, and the good news is –
it does not define you.
Those who refuse to acknowledge that,
stunt your growth,
or keep you in that low vibration
don't belong in your life.
Respect the person you've become.
Honor her.

As humans, we are constantly learning and evolving.
Let go of who you were
so you can transform into a new
self-aware person.

The new person you are growing into
is the who you were meant to be.

You have a beautiful soul,
there's a sparkle in your eyes
that lights up when you speak of things you love,
and that shows how much of a passionate person you are.
You love deeply and intensely,
and you can heat up any room with your potent sexuality
that you gatekeep but is subtlety noticeable.
There's an intensity
that burns within you and
is always brimming beneath the surface.
But most of all,
you are full of love and tenderness.
You can calm anyone who falls into your arms
because your energy is healing and nurturing.
You are a healer, a witch, a goddess, a queen.

God,
thank you for clearing the roads for me,
for paving the way with gold
by removing people, jobs, and situations
not in alignment with my integrity
and my character.
Thank you for removing those
whose intentions were not genuine or pure;
the hypocrites, the snakes
who smiled in my face
but spoke ill behind my back.
Thank you for protecting me,
for the small miracles in my life,
for the strength to start all over,
and for the tough lessons
that only made me come out stronger and wiser.

Memories of Rio

I was in a foreign land
where the smell of barbecue
lingers above rooftops
where the beach matches the sky
and one can stare deeply into both infinities
where the Colombian hippy kissed me on the cheek
and I could smell the marijuana on his dreads
where I bought a dreamcatcher
from the Chilean bohemian
who smelled like armpits.
Where I walked through the sand of Ipanema
and felt so close to the glow of the sunset
I could walk over the ocean
into the aura of pastels painted across the sky
and listen to the soothing hum of the salty currents.

Costa Rica

You need to lose yourself in nature
to realize what is truly important in life.
Pure life is finding happiness in the little things
It's being conscious that the greatest pleasures
and the best things in life cannot be bought.
—*I felt pure life in my own soul.*

New beginnings
May this next chapter
bring abundance and prosperity,
my soul tribe,
travel,
luxury,
And living the life I deserve,
my dream life,
a life from which I don't need a vacation.
I don't know what this next chapter brings
but it will be the one where I make all my dreams come true.

Dear Pam,

For the longest time you've struggled with vulnerability. Experiencing betrayal and secret animosity in almost all your friendships and relationships throughout your life has caused you to develop deep-seated trust issues from a very young age. You felt embarrassed about the hardships you faced and have learned to become secretive and private about your traumas except for the few people you would let in. Now you are exposing from the depth of your soul all the sources of pain in your life for all the world to read. There are chapters, moments, poems in this book that resonated with who you were at a certain point in time, but they no longer define you. This book ends at the right time because these chapters are finally being put to rest. They served as the biggest lessons in your life and pushed you to heal so you can become the woman you've always dreamt of becoming. Moving forward everything is going to align for you. There will be happy times, family reunions, new mindsets, maturity, love, and the wisdom and strength to live the life you deserve. The life you've been trying to manifest for years. All your biggest childhood dreams will come true. Your ancestors are proud. Only you know how much they've supported you, how much they've been giving you signs since 2019 to write this book. You've felt them embrace you on nights you felt alone. You felt it in your heart that they rejoiced when you finally took the steps to make this book a reality. After all the years of signs, synchronicities, you finally did it! And you deserve everything coming for you. May the next book be filled with chapters of your new life. Of victory, triumph, abundance and prosperity. Here's to that and success.

about the *author*

Pamela **Alvarez-Macabu** is a Bolivian-Brazilian writer born and raised in New York. Her love for poetry emerged in the first grade, where she would often write poems in her writing notebook. She says they were not very good, but it was the start of her passion for writing. Throughout her education, English was always her favorite subject. In college, upon taking fiction, non-fiction and poetry writing classes and workshops, she finally realized she wanted to be an author. A phrase she lives by is, *"Nada e por Acaso, tudo esta escrito,"* which translates to, "Nothing just happens, it was all written in the stars." She still resides in New York and aspires to write many more books.

9 798885 902717